Windy

By Juniata Rogers

You cannot see the wind.
But you know it is there.
It howls past windows.
It shakes the trees.

The wind can blow your hair away from your face.

The wind often whips leaves around in circles.

Wind can help or harm. It can power a city. It can tear down a town. But where does wind come from?

Wind is moving air. Air is a **gas**. Gasses do not have shapes. They spread out as much as they can. Gas pushes against whatever it touches. This pushing is called **pressure**.

This balloon is very full. The air inside has high pressure.

Hot air balloons use hot air to rise.

When air gets hot, it floats up. That leaves less air near the ground. This creates low pressure. Cool air pushes down. It creates high pressure.

We call a bunch of air traveling together an **air mass**. When two air masses meet, the warmer air rises. The colder air pushes in to replace it. We feel that as wind.

Beaches are often windy places.

The wind must be stronger than a breeze to move these flags.

There are many kinds of wind. **Breezes** are gentle winds. **Gusts** are strong and fast. **Gales** are even stronger.

Windy days can mean a big change in the weather. A windy day can bring a storm. After a storm, the wind can bring clear weather.

A storm is coming in from the ocean.

Tornadoes can form when hot and cold air masses meet.

Sometimes a storm brings wind. **Tornadoes** and **hurricanes** are two types of storms with strong winds.

Sometimes, wind can be used for power. **Wind farms** turn the power of the wind into energy.

The big "fans" on a wind farm are called wind turbines.

Flying a kite on a windy day can be lots of fun!

We can have fun in the wind.
We blow bubbles and fly kites.
What do you like to do on a
windy day?

Glossary

air mass (AYR MASS): A large amount of air of similar temperature and pressure.

breeze (BREEZ): A gentle wind that lasts for more than a few seconds.

gale (GAYL): A very strong, fast wind.

gas (GAS): A gas is what a liquid becomes when it is heated. Gas doesn't hold a shape. It tends to spread out as much as it can.

gust (GUST): A strong but brief burst of wind.

hurricane (HUR-ih-kayn): A windy storm that develops on the ocean. It brings a lot of rain and strong, damaging winds.

pressure (PRESH-ur): The amount of pushing that is happening. Cold air masses tend to have higher air pressure and hot air masses tend to have lower air pressure.

tornado (tor-NAY-doh): A swirling storm of very fast winds. Tornadoes can cause a lot of damage.

wind farm (WIND FARM): A place where windmills convert the power of the wind into energy. The wind blows the blades of the windmill, and the spinning of the blades makes electricity.

To Find Out More

Books

Jensen, Belinda. *Spinning Wind and Water: Hurricanes.* Minneapolis, MN: Millbrook Press, 2016.

Roker, Al. *Al Roker's Extreme Weather: Tornadoes, Typhoons, and Other Weather Phenomena.* New York, NY: HarperCollins, 2017.

VanVoorst, Jenny Fretland. *Wind.* Minneapolis, MN: Millbrook Press, 2016.

Websites

Visit our website for links about wind:
childsworld.com/links

Note to Parents, Teachers, and Librarians: We routinely verify our Web links to make sure they are safe and active sites. So encourage your readers to check them out!

Index

About the Author

Juniata Rogers grew up in Newport, Rhode Island. She has worked as a naturalist, an art model, and a teacher. She's been writing professionally for 25 years, and currently lives near Washington, DC.

The Child's World
childsworld.com

Published by The Child's World®
1980 Lookout Drive • Mankato, MN 56003-1705
800-599-READ • www.childsworld.com

Photo credits: Africa Studio/Shutterstock.com: 20; andreiuc88/Shutterstock.com: 4; ArtisticPhoto/Shutterstock.com: 12; Cheryl Casey/Shutterstock.com: cover, 1; Drew McArthur/Shutterstock.com: 15; juninatt/Shutterstock.com: 3; Minerva Studio/Shutterstock.com: 16; nikkytok/Shutterstock.com: 7; pongpinun traisrisilp/Shutterstock.com: 8; S Curtis/Shutterstock.com: 11; WDG Photo/Shutterstock.com: 19

ISBN Hardcover: 9781503827936
ISBN Paperback: 9781622434619
LCCN: 2018939781

Printed in the United States of America • PA02398